MW00849155

Floodlight Press

Orlando, Florida

ISBN-13:

978-0692424537

ISBN-10:

0692424539

Defining The Executive Pastor Role

Book One

In The Backstage Pastors Series

By Phil Taylor

Copyright © 2015

Phil Taylor

First Edition

1.4

ABOUT THE BACKSTAGE PASTORS BOOK SERIES

The Backstage Pastors series of books have been designed to target specific topics with enough depth to provide meaningful direction but with brevity that facilitates reading or skimming quickly. My hope is to put extremely practical tools into your hands at a reasonable cost that will quickly *train you up* so that you are quickly *freed up* to continue with the demands of life and ministry.

I've chosen to publish these books on Amazon for multiple reasons. One key driver is that this platform allows me the freedom to regularly tweak, update and expand these works. In essence, the book never has to be done. With that in mind, I invite you to take notes and send me your thoughts at backstagepastors@gmail.com. Who knows, maybe the next edition will include your insight or question!

Find information about my pastoral coaching, consulting and speaking, as well as new articles on practical topics at www.backstagepastors.com. Continue the conversation online by using #backstagepastors.

TABLE OF CONTENTS

FOREWARD

By Mike Bonem

When Roger Patterson and I wrote *Leading from the Second Chair*, we frequently described the book as the start of a conversation about what it means to lead effectively in this challenging role. One of the first people to engage in that conversation was Phil Taylor.

When Phil reached out to me more than 10 years ago, my reaction was, "Huh?" Like Nathanael being told that the Messiah had arrived and was from Nazareth, I wondered if it was possible for Troy, New York to have a church with an executive pastor. Fortunately, I moved beyond my misguided Bible-belt biases and began a conversation with Phil that has continued over these many years.

I could say that the conversation has lasted this long because Phil had so much to learn, but that would be a terrible misrepresentation. Phil is indeed an eager learner, but the truth is that even then, he demonstrated great wisdom as an executive pastor. Over the years, he has continued to learn and grow, and eventually moved to Orlando where a larger church and a more complex role awaited. Like any good leader, he has also given an increasing amount of his energy to influencing and equipping others.

That's where *Defining the Role of the Executive Pastor* enters the picture, as well as the other books that will follow in the Backstage Pastors series. It's Phil's opportunity to share some of what he has learned with you. As you read the pages that follow, you'll be challenged to wrestle with the job description of an executive pastor. What responsibilities are involved in this role and what qualities are essential for those who want to succeed? Phil also does an outstanding job in unpacking the "deep-wide paradox." That's the term that Roger and I coined to describe the challenge of working at the 50,000 foot level with a visionary leader and concurrently hovering close to the ground with staff members and volunteers who are charged with turning that vision into reality.

What I'm most excited about, however, is that you will get a taste of Phil's passion and deep sense of calling to the second chair. He knows that the executive pastor role is vital for churches of many different sizes. He knows that he is uniquely gifted for this job. And in these realities, he finds joy and enthusiasm that stands in stark contrast to the old line that "second chair is second best." Phil's ministry and this book give testimony to a very different truth.

I'm thankful that Phil joined our conversation a decade ago, and I'm even more thankful that he is now expanding the circle of friends that will enter into the dialogue about second chair leadership. As you engage in that conversation, I'm convinced that more churches will live into their Kingdom potential because of the gifts of second chair leaders like you.

Mike Bonem

Consultant and coach, co-author of *Leading from the Second Chair*

www.mikebonem.com

"It has been said that an institution is the lengthening shadow of a visionary leader. What rarely is said is that in the shadow of that visionary leader was another leader who executed the primary leader's ideas, monitored the budgets, built the infrastructure and systems, and, along the way, cleaned up a few of the messes. Such is the life of a leader who is "second in command".

-Bruce Hornsby[i]

INTRODUCTION

Is it really possible to define the Executive Pastor role when there are so many variables involved? How do you deal with the fact that every church seems to give the second in command a different job description? How does the personality of the Lead Pastor affect the definition of the Executive Pastor? Where do skill set, education, and experience of the Executive Pastor fit in? What about church size? What about leadership or government structure and the traditions of a particular church? Do cultural differences matter? Does denominational affiliation matter? The Second-In-Command role is perhaps the most misunderstood position on the entire church staff. As a result, it becomes difficult to define the second chair role.

The problem gets even more complicated when you realize that there is little consistency of the actual job titles that the "second-in-command" use from church to church. Some Associate Pastors are really Executive Pastors. Some Executive Pastors are more like Operations Directors. Some large churches have shifted the Executive Pastor title to Lead Pastor of something or other, thus creating a system with multiple Lead Pastors. Other churches list multiple

Executive Pastors over various departments making it difficult to say who is truly the *Second-In-Command*.

Regardless of what the business card says, my focus in this book is on that critical Second-In-Command Pastor in the church . . . the Second Chair Leader . . . the right hand man. I happen to like the title "Executive Pastor," or "XP" for short-hand, so I'll stick with that. Call it what you want in your church. I don't think it matters that much from an eternal perspective and at the end of the day, we will all cast our titles and any other crowns we've acquired on this sin-soaked planet before our King, so let's just get to work.

While our role in the grand scheme of church history is relatively small, there is much to do while we are still breathing, and we ought to do our jobs to the best of our ability. This short book is designed to put a simple, laser focused, and accessible tool into your hands right away. This is not the magic bullet book on the Second Chair role. This is meant to be a starting point for those wrestling with their calling and those entering a new phase of complexity in their church leadership. If you are currently a second-in-command leader but you lack definition, this book will point you in the right direction. If you are praying about entering an Executive Pastor role, this book will help you figure out if that is the right path for you to take. If you are a Lead Pastor who is considering hiring an Executive Pastor, you will find this book helpful as you process that major decision.

To quote the T-Shirt I once saw on the back of an Apple Store employee: "Sometimes, the foundation is in the back of the house". I can't help but see the correlation to the Second Chair Pastor in the church. My hope is that in the following pages, you would be encouraged and equipped to build a stronger foundation for your church by enhancing the vision of your Lead Pastor and, therefore, pointing more people to Jesus Christ. Let's see what the Spirit can do through us.

Let's get into this.

"Everyone has a plan, till they get punched in the face."

-Mike Tyson

CHAPTER ONE

Becoming A Backstage Pastor

When I was a senior in college, my roommates and I decided to take a spring-break trip together. We were not the type of students that longed for alcohol infused debauchery in some sun soaked destination filled with equally drunk, scantily clad college girls dancing on an MTV stage. We knew our sin natures enough to avoid such places. Instead we went to my parents' house, which, at the time, was a train ride away from downtown Boston. We did all the usual site-seeing as cheaply as possible, but decided to splurge on last minute discount tickets to *Les Miserables*. I think we had all just taken a literature class and were flying high on our new found sense of cultural snobbery. So, we went to the will-call desk, showed our student ID's and were treated to a great, last minute price on amazing seats for Victor Hugo's masterpiece.

As I sat there watching the spectacle that is *the theatre* all I could think of was . . . *there must be someone behind the scenes making all of this run perfectly?* Rather than be impressed with the skill of the actors and actresses or the sweeping musical score or the intricacy with which the sets were built, all I wanted to know was . . . **Who is** *running this thing? Who makes sure that everyone is in the right place at the right time? Who calls the under-study when the main actor gets the flu? Who deals with squabbles between the people on stage and the people in the orchestra pit? **Who is in charge backstage?*** As the music intensified, I had this light bulb realization moment that churches would probably run more effectively if they too had someone *backstage,* so to speak, handling all the details, so that the people *on stage* could focus on the task at hand. At the time, I had no idea that this role was just starting to gain steam in America's largest churches under the job title "Executive Pastor".

But of course, I was a product of the church culture that I had come of age in—a culture where the only job on a church staff worth pursuing was the Lead or Senior Pastor role. As a result, it took me over seven years to finally land in that second chair in a newly forming church plant, seated next to a classic creative-communicator-visionary-type of Lead Pastor who probably would not have gotten his vision off the ground in the same way had he not gathered a team around him that included someone who thrived on seeing the details amidst the big picture and keeping both in balance.

This idea of "coming along side of" in a subordinate manner is at the core of the Executive Pastor role. Roger Patterson points to Timothy and says that, *"Timothy is one* of the clearest examples of subordinate leadership found in the New Testament. *In him is found the complete picture of serving under the authority of another and being granted authority to lead and serve.*[ii] Paul includes him in greetings and salutations and calls him a "true son" (1 Timothy 1:2). Paul trusted Timothy and could therefore give him free reign to implement the vision. Even Jesus spent his life pointing people to the Father! We are in good company when we choose a life of subordination.

The problem was that while I was comfortable with being second and even knew I wanted to be *that guy* behind the scenes—making it all come together efficiently—I had very little to lean on other than my own intuition and related experience in the business world. I searched for books and articles on the Executive Pastor role but found very little to aid in my education and development. I met with the executive pastor at a local mega-church but found that his mainstream wisdom regarding giant facilities and budgets in the multi-millions was often hard to apply to our indie-rock style church plant meeting in a rented bar/nightclub complete with frozen puke on the sidewalks every cold Sunday morning. (I did, however, find myself returning to what I learned from him several years later when I became the Executive Pastor of Leadership and Development in a large multi-site mega-church). I also found that my pastoral

DNA did not always match up with the more business oriented XP's who seemed to dominate the role. In short, I wanted to learn, but I was hard-pressed to find many opportunities to do so[iii].

Early in my first church plant, as we were just starting to bump up against that coveted "200 person mark", I found myself traveling to Michigan to meet with a large multi-site congregation that wanted to support our new church financially. I was excited to have lunch with my counterpart there, eager to learn whatever I could. However, I was surprised when I realized that this XP serving a church of over 10,000 saw this time as an opportunity to get connected to a young upstart church planter who had not yet had the chance to become jaded with the struggles of ministry. (I pray that I have that same wisdom and willingness to learn from younger generations as I progress through the second half of my life!)

As *he* barraged *me* with questions, I finally said "Kyle, what could you possibly learn from me? I'm in this tiny church that's not even two years old. Your paid staff is bigger than our average Sunday attendance!" He responded very matter of factly saying . . . *"Phil, you and I do the exact same thing, I just do it with more zero's at the end."*[iv] His openness to listen freed me up to share with him all the thoughts that had been swirling in my head regarding this second-chair role that I was falling in love with. I gushed all of my rookie theories about XP/LP relationships and told him of my dreams of connecting with other XP's throughout my region and bringing them together so that we could learn from one another. I probably seemed like a new kindergarten kid at the end of his first day of school, all excited about his classroom, his teacher, his new friends, the lunchroom, playground and art class! And to be honest, that *is* kind of how I felt. After lunch, as we drove back to the church building, Kyle turned to me and said, *"So, when are you going to start writing all this stuff down for others to benefit from?"* I pointed out once again that our church was less than two years old, and my experience in the XP role was only slightly longer if you counted the pre-launch phase. With a seriousness that felt like a word from God, Kyle turned to me and said, *"No Phil, you have a unique voice here, and you need to share that, you need to write."*

On the plane ride home from Detroit, I found myself writing feverishly on any scrap of paper I could find, trying to capture all that I sensed God was calling me to say. Since then I have taken every opportunity I could to spend time with executive pastors of all types: young, old, rookies, deeply experienced, business background, seminary background, large church, small church, multi-site, and all different denominations and networks. At times, I have been the one doing the learning. At other times, God has pushed me to serve others that are less experienced in the role. I've also taken opportunities to teach or lead discussions at conferences hosted by our church-planting network[v]. I've gathered with XP's locally, regionally and nationally in cohort style learning environments. I've searched out every possible book, article, blog entry and lecture related to the second chair role in the church. When I realized that the list is no more than a page long I expanded my search to every secular counterpart I could come up with: COO, VP, Chief Of Staff, first mate, whatever I could find that *seemed* like second-in-command. I've even sought out examples from classic literature and pop culture out of desperation to wrap my brain around the *Second-Chair role*. And of course, I have poured over any scripture that appeared to speak to the Executive Pastor—all in an effort to discover what it means to be a pastor who primarily exists *off-stage* . . . *backstage*.

It's been an amazing ride. It is incredibly freeing to know exactly where you fit best in the church. If you are finding yourself getting excited as you read this thinking "wow, this is totally me. I'm not the only crazy one after all," I pray that you find great clarity on your future in God's work on this planet.

"General, you have the difficult task of reducing chaos to order."

-General-in-chief George B. McClellen (to General Halleck, Abraham Lincoln's second in command.)[vi]

CHAPTER TWO

From Chaos To Order

A lot of people are confused when I tell them I'm an Executive Pastor. They assume that I'm primarily working with numbers, graphs and administrative oversight. That is certainly a part of my job, but if that was all I did, any guy with an MBA and a calculator could be an Executive Pastor.

If you boil it all down, my role as Executive **Pastor** (emphasis on pastor) is to oversee the effective implementation of the vision of the church. The vision and direction of a church are cast largely by the Lead Pastor. That's his key role. He casts that vision from the pulpit, in key leadership development sessions, and in a thousand other ways. But if he gets bogged down in implementing that vision, it tends to kill the artistic creativity of the visionary leader—it burns him out. Additionally, many Lead Pastors tend to think in terms of, "Step 1 . . . step 100"[vii]. They often have little knowledge or passion for how you go about actually taking a vision *from* step 1 to step 100. Steps two through ninety-nine are kind of boring to them. And for this reason, many great ideas fall to the ground unused, like fruit in an abandoned orchard.

So who is best suited to implement the vision of the lead pastor? It takes another person with a pastoral heart and mind to keep his eyes, hands, heart and soul on *every* part of the ministry at *all* times in *some* sense. The Executive Pastor becomes the guy who not only *implements* the vision but also *protects* it. This is especially important in large or fast growing churches where everyone assumes that *someone else* is taking care of . . . [insert undone job]. **Somebody** has to have the whole organization in mind while continuing to zoom in on very specific details. And *somebody* has to be able to take the Lead Pastor's vision and break it into manageable bites for the scores of people who will implement those tiny little pieces of the larger puzzle.

An intimate understanding of the vision is critical in leading well from the second-chair. The Executive Pastor has to be able to take a pile of ideas and aspirations and reverse engineer them into a plan of attack. A friend and former XP at Sojourn Church in Louisville, KY noted that, *"I can't **do** the vision of the church if I'm not **in** the vision conversations early on."*[viii] In order for another pastor to be in on those early vision conversations, he has to have a certain level of leadership maturity to handle an unformed idea and not rush too quickly to matters of budget and HR.

For fun, I love to study architecture. (I know, I'm weird. Most XP's are.) So, let's say you are a famous architect like Frank Gehry, the Canadian responsible designing whimsical masterpieces like the Guggenheim Museum in Bibao, Spain, the Stata center at MIT and the Walt Disney Concert Hall in L.A. Let's say Frank Gehry has been asked to design an art gallery. First, he meets with his clients and gets a feel for what they need in a building. Then, he does some research and thinking and brooding over the purpose of this building he's been asked to design. He imagines people walking through the doors. He sees museum patrons in the lobby taking in the expansive space figuring out where to go first. He imagines eating lunch with them in the café, walking with them through the museum shop and ending their day where they began, in the lobby. He wants them to *feel* a certain way, have certain emotions and experiences as they turn this corner or that corner. He even thinks of how the outside of the building will interact with surrounding buildings or landscapes. The architect has *created a vision* for a future building . . . in this case, an art gallery.

Gehry then picks up his colored pencils and sits down at his drafting table and goes to work. In the end, it looks like a beautiful mess of curvy lines and scribbled concepts (seriously . . . google Frank Gehry and you'll see what I mean). Somehow from this mess, we get sculpted works of art that architecture geeks seek out while on vacation (much

t and chagrin of their family). We see
ıe) and then we see his buildings (step
:ritically important to note that the Lead
handle steps two through ninety-nine in
great ᴜᴇᴛᴜ.   early on, he hands those scribbled
drawings and cryptic directions off to another architect,
someone who is able to take the mess and put it into a form
that can be handed to construction workers, steel craftsmen
and engineers. Gehry will certainly step in from time to time,
steering the project here and there, causing little course
corrections in the direction of the building plans to maintain
the purity of his initial vision. But by and large, once the
vision has been cast, he is out of the picture and on to the
next project. Other architects take over in speaking *for* him,
continuing to cast vision—*Gehry's vision*—in a pure way,
while implementing that vision with a team of specialists in
everything from fire code safety to lighting and flooring
design.

This secondary architect is the Executive Pastor in the
church. The visionary leadership of the Lead Pastor serves as
a rally-call, a catalyst, a fire-igniter. But when the pep rally
is over and everyone is ready to move, you've got to have a
plan in place, and that plan has to have some teeth to it or
people will be confused and lose momentum. That's where

the second chair guys get to shine. That's where *order* emerges from *chaos*.

But What If My Lead Pastor Is Not Like the Ones You Describe?

The reality is that not all Lead Pastors are crazy-big vision dreamers. Therefore, your role may not be so focused on the LP. Bonem and Patterson put a base level call on the XP by saying that you are *"a person in a subordinate role whose influence with others adds value throughout the organization."[ix]* So even if your Lead Pastor is not a big vision dreamer, you can still add tremendous value throughout the organization. An Executive Pastor could be named or hired for any number of reasons, here are three common ones:

1. The Lead Pastor needs a right hand man. In this case, the XP's job is LP focused, and the LP is the primary and most immediate beneficiary.

2. The church or board has identified that they need someone to run things more effectively behind the scenes. In this case, the XP's job is church or board focused and the primary beneficiary is the church, or perhaps a non-staff board.

3. The church wants to retain or attract a particular leader by giving him an executive level role in recognition of his experience or gifting. In this case, the XP's job is XP focused and the immediate beneficiary is the XP. This is especially true for the XP who hopes to one day be an LP, and may even have been hired as the heir apparent for an aging Lead Pastor.

Understanding why you were hired really does drive the direction of the your role and even how you manage your schedule. Personally, I prefer to work in scenario one, under a highly gifted communicator-visionary who is in need of a second-in-command to help him implement his vision. I write with that perspective in mind. But I recognize that you may find yourself working under scenario two or three and will need to adapt what you read here.

Some Thoughts on Risk and the Second Chair Leader.

As we seek to bring order out of chaotically beautiful ideas, there is a temptation to eliminate the element of risk in your church. While risky behavior might be expected, even praised in a visionary Lead Pastor, second chair leaders are not always known for being risk takers. In one sense, it's that very quality that makes us a great balance to our riskier LP counterparts. And yet, we have to know when to make a bet. We have to know when to step out in faith.

Several years ago, I realized that many of the best experiences in my life came about because I put aside my *risk averseness* and stepped off the ledge so to speak, not knowing exactly if I would fall or fly! When I decided to chase after the woman I was falling in love with in college, I took a risk. I could have been rejected (in fact I was . . . at first). When I chose a seminary with the reputation of being very difficult, I took a risk. I could have failed out (and nearly did). When I chose to leave my comfortable, established suburban church for an urban church plant, I took a risk. We could have failed like the vast majority of church plants. When I left my geographical sphere of influence in the Northeast for a church in Florida, I took a risk.

Risk is not something that comes naturally to me, but I've learned that I need to take risks—at least calculated risks—because it forces me to rely on God instead of my well-thought-out plans. Being risk averse is a common trait for XP types. We are often the balance to our crazy visionary lead pastors. Therefore, our risk aversion is not seen as a negative, but rather a sought after positive trait. We are expected to be the counter weight to the off-the-wall ideas that are not feasible in any sense of the word. Yet, there are times for each of us when we must get past our cautious, steady personalities and step out in faith on some crazy idea that just might work. We must get past ourselves and our natural aversion to risk and get on board with where God may be calling us and the ministries we serve.

Several years ago, my wife and I were getting ready to make a major ministry move. While we knew we were being called to it, it still felt like a huge risk to me. I remember lying in bed with Aimee one night and saying "What if it doesn't work? What if it all comes crashing down? What if this is a complete failure?" And my wife just looked at me and said: "Obedience is never failure". She was right.

So, as you seek to bring order out of chaos, don't be so quick to eliminate *all* the chaos. Don't get rid of *all* the risk. Some risk is good for your journey of trust. Some chaos will keep you from becoming small-mindedly weird, just like some germs keep your immune system healthy. Managing the risk is fine; eliminating it altogether is not. There is a difference between failure caused by ignorance and failure caused by negligence.

"There is tension embedded in the "executive pastor" title. Sometimes what an "executive" *would* do in a situation and what a "pastor" *must* do contradict each other. In those moments, "pastor" must trump "executive.""[x]

-Eric Geiger

CHAPTER THREE

Does the Second-In-Command Need to be a Pastor?

Lot's of people think that the Second-In-Command is just the guy on the team who is kind of OCD and gets a little breathy when he sees a good Excel spread sheet. There is so much more to it than that. He has to be someone who can sit down with a key leader in the church and help that person figure out how they will take the larger vision of the church and bring it down to the men's ministry, or the security team or the guest connection team, or the building project, or the budget. The process of *bringing vision into reality* is different than the initial creativity involved in casting the vision for the church as a whole, but it still involves creativity. The guy who picks up where Frank Gehry leaves off kind of *has to be an architect* as well (see chapter 2), or else the vision will not be translated properly due to a language gap. Likewise, the guy who picks up where the lead pastor leaves off kind of has to be pastor as well—someone who will understand the theological, spiritual and practical ramifications of the vision that is being cast—someone who will see ahead three chess moves to the pastoral needs that will be created by the unveiling of this vision—someone who has internalized the Lead Pastor's vision so deep in his core that he will defend it and protect it like it is his own. This is the role of the Executive Pastor who comes alongside of a visionary Lead Pastor and says "I'm with you—I'm ready to go to battle for what God has called you to do in and through this church."

When God revealed His will for church leadership through the Apostle Paul, he called them Elders (used interchangeably in the New Testament with "Pastor", "Bishop", "Overseer" and "Shepherd"). The books of First Timothy and Titus gave us the outline and character qualifications for these pastor/elders along with a few notes on the skill set required to do the job well.[xi] In our 21st century western context of multi-site and multi-staffed churches, we have rightly specialized our leadership to be more effective at reaching our cultures with the gospel of Jesus Christ, but the baseline idea remains the same. The people driving the mission and vision of the church need to be elder qualified if they are going to speak and lead with the authority that God intended them to have. I don't see the upside in giving a high-level leadership role in the church to a person with no potential for meeting the biblical qualifications of an elder! I don't care how gifted a man is; if there are things in his life that would disqualify him from being an Elder/Pastor, he should not occupy the second chair role. It does not matter if someone was the CEO, CFO, or

COO of a Fortune 500 company, if the Apostle Paul could never have appointed that person to the highest office in the church, the role of Elder, neither should we, no matter where the MBA is from. If he does not have a deep and abiding understanding of the Gospel, he is nothing more than a purveyor of religious goods and services.

What if a person is not quite ready to be an Elder/Pastor?

Ideally, a person is already elder qualified *and* commissioned (ordained, licensed, recognized, whatever your church calls it) before becoming an Executive Pastor, but this is not always possible, especially in smaller churches. I often find myself coaching Lead Pastors who really want an Executive Pastor. They will tell me they have identified someone in their congregation or staff with strong administrative, organizational and strategic thinking skills and they think he might make a good second-chair leader, even though he is not currently an Elder/Pastor. I always counsel these LP's to really do a gut check.   Ask yourself: Could you ever see this person as an Elder/Pastor? Will the church ever see this person as a pastor? Will the other Elders/Pastors respect this person as a peer? Would you want your daughter to marry this guy if they were the same age? If the answer is no to any of these questions, then he should not even be considered. But if the answer is "Yes, however, he needs some work", then proceed with caution . . . but do proceed.

Special Note for Lead Pastors:

Give developing pastors added *responsibility*, but limited *authority*. A nice long two-year eldership development process allows you to move someone forward without prematurely committing yourself to an org chart you might regret later. Don't succumb to the temptation to fast-track a future pastor just because you enjoy grabbing a beer with him, or you think you really need his help *right now*. After a year or so, you could begin to call him an "Elder-In-Process", and at the end of the second year, you can make him an official Elder/Pastor. In the meantime, call him a director, or coordinator or anything really. Just don't call him a pastor until he is truly ready to wear that mantle. If you do decide to call this young, untested guy a pastor because your church polity has pastors that are not Elders, that's OK, just go slow on giving him the authority of a voting Elder.

Guard the Elder/Pastor title carefully because it is much easier to *increase* the authority and leadership level of someone on staff than it is to *reduce* it. If a person retains a title like "Executive Director" while they study, learn and develop, they can be promoted easily to Executive Pastor when the time is right. I've never regretted going slow with someone in leadership development, but I have regretted going to quickly. It is much harder to go back and demote someone because you've found out that he may never be Elder/Pastor qualified, even though he brings real value to the team. How do you explain to a congregation that Pastor Tim is no longer a pastor but he's in the same role, doing a lot of the same job? It's much easier move Tim to a different role and hire or train up his boss if the growth of the church requires such a move. Again, guard the Elder/Pastor title carefully. There is a reason why the scriptures tell us "Do not lay hands on an Elder too hastily" (1 Tim. 5:22). In the midst of all of this muddy and delicate leadership development, don't forget to pastor the people you are training up to be pastors. They will learn a great deal from you through how you treat them.

I believe that leadership development is one of the most important things to get right in a church. So much hangs on having the right people in the right roles. Let's stick with what the Bible seems to say and have our very top leaders be Elder/Pastor qualified so that they are able to serve and pastor well.

"When we're able to put most of our energy into developing our natural talents, extraordinary room for growth exists. So, a revision to the "You-can-be-anything-you-want-to-be" maxim might be more accurate: You cannot be anything you want to be—but you can be a lot more of who you already are."

-Tom Rath[xii]

CHAPTER FOUR

Discovering your Origin of Leadership:

Are you a capital "E" or a capital "P"?

There are certain criteria we can establish when it comes to the make-up or DNA of Pastors. They have to meet the qualifications for Elders found in 1 Timothy and Titus—that much we know for sure (see chapter three). Everything else that goes beyond that is nothing more than the distinct cultural needs for the church in your context and time period. And that's okay . . . I don't think it's wrong to have all sorts of pastoral titles that the apostles never imagined like "Pastor of Technology" or "Executive Pastor" or "Pastor of Funtivities" as one of our Student Ministry staff suggested his title should be at Mosaic Church. It's fine to invent new pastoral roles as long as we keep what we find in scripture as the baseline. Most of what we find in scripture for elder qualifications is character based, not ability based.

Throughout my years in the Executive Pastor role, I've had the privilege of getting to know many of my peers in ministry. At the risk of oversimplification, I have noticed that most XPs fall into one of two categories, and this often dictates the direction and emphasis of the XP's ministry. This is really important, so pay attention here! Most Executive Pastors will either be an **Executive** pastor with a capital "E" and lower case "p", or, they will be an executive **Pastor** with a lower case "e" and a capital "P". Does that make sense? Executive Pastors seem to always *lean on* one side or the other and we often *lead out of* this tendency. We either lead as *Executives* who happen to be serving in a pastoral role or as *Pastors* who happen to be serving in an executive role. This is what I call your *Origin of Leadership*. The question I want to help you ask is this: "Am I a "Capital E" guy, or a "Capital P" guy?"

It has been my experience that the guy who leaves the business world to become an XP will typically lean on the Executive side of the equation, while the guy who primarily has a vocational ministry background or education will lean towards the Pastor side[xiii]. Both are effective at what they do but will obviously do the job differently, and each will bring their own strengths and weaknesses to the table.

The capital "E" guys will gravitate towards policies and procedures and find themselves issuing memos on the number of sodas and juice the staff may consume in one day from the office kitchen[xiv]. The capital "P" guys will find themselves enjoying counseling and shepherding in the midst of what was intended to be a performance evaluation meeting. The capital "E" guys will enjoy a more hands on approach to managing things like human resources, budgeting and capital campaigns while the capital "P" guys will find the experts in those areas and lean on them, functioning in more of a *catalyst* role. The capital "E" guys will likely have an intimate knowledge and love of Excel formulas, while the capital "P" guys will be trying to figure if they have time to teach a theology class on the side.

So is one better than the other? Well, our pride would tell us that whatever type of XP *I am* is the *best* kind of XP. I don't think that's right. Don't forget that administration is a supernatural gift from the Holy Spirit! I think the better question to ask is "Which type of XP does my church need?" I am convinced that the XP's job title and skill set must have a complimentary relationship to the Lead Pastor's job title and skill set. So when I ask: "Which type of XP does your church need?" what I really mean is "Which type of XP does your LP need?"

There are Lead Pastors who preach 50 times a year because that is their greatest passion in ministry. An Executive Pastor working with a guy like that probably does not need to be as strong in the pulpit as someone working with a Lead Pastor who only wants to preach 40 times a year. There are LP's who genuinely enjoy taking the vision of the church and breaking it down into manageable pieces to be implemented. An Executive Pastor working with that guy probably does not need to be *as strong* of a system's analyst as someone in another situation.

What about daily pastoral work? Interestingly, many LP's will tell you that they are not what you would describe as a "people person." It's just not their strong suit. The first Lead Pastor that I worked for commented *during a sermon* that he never understood why God had called a certifiable *misanthrope* to be a pastor![xv] That LP needs an XP who truly enjoys shepherding and pastoring the people. This is especially true in churches under a 1,000 people where a good percentage of the core church has some personal connection to *one of* the pastors. Some LP's will want to be very involved with the staff, while others will want to deal solely with the Executive Team as his only direct reports and let the rest of the staff report to the XP. Some quixotic LP's will skip out on staff meetings altogether to make a key hospital visit, while others are more than happy to delegate pastoral visits to others with a chaplain personality. These are the kinds of indicators one needs to discern in determining what type of XP a church (and it's Lead Pastor) really need.

I'm not suggesting here that the job of the XP is to simply do everything that the LP does not want or like to do. Rather, what I'm suggesting is that the First Chair and

Second Chair should have a unique symbiotic working relationship—different and more critical than any other staff relationship. I believe it is best when the LP and XP *balance each other out* so that the weaknesses of one, meets the strengths of the other. This allows you to *call each other out* when personality and giftedness become an excuse. It also allows you to *help each other out* in seeing the church through the unique lens that each pastor has been gifted with. In essence, opposites not only attract, but also make for a stronger leadership team.[xvi]

But even after you figure all this out and get the right team in place, there will still be gaps. So what do you do when the giftedness of the XP still falls short of the full needs of the church?

1. *Staff to Your Weaknesses*

Don't be afraid to hit the ceiling in a particular area of your stated tasks. It's OK to say you are not the ultimate best fit for some parts of your job. An XP will naturally lead from his strongest suit most of the time. So, if you are an XP and you know what side you fall on here (capital E or capital P) . . . should you simply resign yourself to leading and working out of those areas only and let our organizations be weak in the alternating areas? *Absolutely not!* This is not an either/or question. There are two things we can do when we grasp and embrace our *origin of leadership*. **First, we can staff to our weaknesses** through hiring staff or recruiting key volunteers to fit the size and needs of your church.

Too often we look at the other pastors in our lives and we think "well, he's really good at . . . whatever . . . so I should be too." But that's just silly. God has made you exactly the way he wanted you, and he has called us to do life in community. It's called "the body of Christ," you don't have to be every part on that body. Nor should you even try. Staffing to your weakness is just good body theology.

For example, in a church that I co-planted in NY, I managed to have a pretty good grasp on all aspects of budgeting, spending, offerings, etc. for the first few years of our existence. I knew however that, ultimately, it would become critical that someone else with a stronger accounting background and more financial acumen would take on the stewardship side of the church. An XP with a capital "E" business background might have been able to stay in that role longer, but that was not me. I could easily think through the big picture of how our budget matched up with our core values and staffing decisions. I enjoyed building strategies for capital expenditures, multi-site budgeting and facility expansion. But I needed someone else to get into the numbers at a granular level to produce reports and analysis that then fed into bigger budgetary decisions. Years later, when I stepped into a much larger church, I felt confident doing so because they already had an Executive Director of Operations who would be strong where I was weak. I know my *origin of leadership*. I'm a capital "P" guy, and I'm good with that! I know my strengths and weaknesses and that frees me up to serve the church well in the areas where I can be most helpful and simply say no to opportunities that will set me and the church up for failure.

I was talking with an XP at a church in Michigan that, at the time, was running about 10,000 people on average in attendance. I was asking him what his philosophy of leadership in the church was, and he said "I don't run the church like a well oiled machine, I run it like a well watered garden."[xvii] Do you think he loved the business side of his mega church? NO! That's why he hired a business manager and a stewardship pastor and facilities managers, and on and on it went. Staffing to your weakness becomes critical as you recognize your *origin of leadership*.

How Does This Work In Smaller Churches?

While I enjoy the benefits of having a large church staff today, I remember all too well what it was like to lean solely on volunteers for the things that I was not good at. If you are an XP in a church of under 1000 people, you may not have the opportunity to utilize paid staff to offset your weaknesses, but that doesn't necessarily mean you have to rely on volunteers. Some things can be outsourced entirely in a fairly cost effective manner, such as lower-level accounting, paying the bills, etc. However, other areas will need to be handed off to trusted lay-elders, deacons, key volunteers or non-paid staff. If you have a godly, mature woman who is passionate about women's ministry, you can hand that off to her and give her direction as needed. If you have a retired CEO who enjoyed a successful career, you can task him with all sorts of strategic areas in the church. If you are blessed to have a retired pastor in your midst, by all means, put that man to work overseeing visitation, or prayer ministry, or counseling, or other things that fire him up!

Don't be afraid to hand off key roles in the church by building your top volunteer team. In fact, this may be the best way that you can spend your time in the church. Even in smaller churches, a good Second-Chair leader is constantly working himself out of a job, which in turn, frees him up to work on other areas of the church that need careful attention. The side benefit of this approach is that as your church grows and your staff needs to grow, you may never need to go outside your walls to hire new people. You may be able to just move a ten-hour a week volunteer into a thirty-hour a week part-time staffer as the needs of his or her ministry area grow. Internal hires go a long way to ensuring a cultural fit, vision and mission alignment, and the intangible need to actually like the people you work with!

2. Become Friends With Executive Pastors Who Are Different Than You.

The second key thing that you can do to compensate for areas of weakness is to create friendships with other XP's who are strong where you tend to be weak. Different types of XPs will help you grow in the areas where you are weak. See, you don't have to know how to make a great excel spreadsheet, but you do need to understand how to read one. For example, if you don't know what it means when there is a parenthesis around a number, you are in rough shape as an XP! You don't need to have a thorough understanding of contract law, but you do need to be able to make sense of the lease on a building.

Unless you live in the middle of nowhere, there are probably other XP's in your geographical area. Find one that is the opposite of you and befriend him. A capital "P" guy needs to have a buddy who is a capital "E" guy and vice-versa. If you find yourself serving in the XP role of a smaller church, do not hesitate to call or e-mail the guy in your local mega-church. The XP in a church of 10,000 people will likely answer your email more quickly than the LP in a church of 200. It's not that XP's have nothing else to do, it's just that unlike high profile Lead Pastors, the XP may not get that many emails or calls from people outside of their church asking for their advice and input. As a result, they are glad to hear from another XP and excited to share what they have learned.

Early in my career as an XP, I benefited greatly from a man who was extremely different than me in terms of personality and background.[xviii] We were both Executive Pastors, and there was a lot of overlap in our daily lives as XPs, but our strengths and weaknesses were dead opposite. By leaning on and learning from his strengths, I was able to compensate for some areas where I was weak. Investing in relationships with other XPs will pay huge dividends over the years.

3. Create an Executive Pastor Roundtable

Over time, I developed friendships with many different types of Executive Pastors, each having his own strengths and expertise. As such, I learned to rely on each of them in different ways. I learned which ones to call when I was thinking through a new policy or structural change. I learned who to call with HR matters, facility issues, legal challenges, technology roadblocks, etc. I figured out who had more experience and knowledge than me, and I sought those people out, paid for their lunch and learned a lot. Over time I was able to feed back into that circle of friends as my own skill and experience grew. Eventually, I created an Executive Pastor Roundtable or Cohort style gathering. To quote my six year old sons current favorite movie: *"Everything is awesome, everything is cool when your part of a team."*[xix]

Interestingly, while many Executive Pastors want this sort of interaction with other Second-Chair Leaders, they are not always proactive about seeking it out. As a result, I have consistently worked to create an Executive Pastor Roundtable wherever I have lived. We'll meet quarterly, or bi-monthly for fellowship and guided discussions that address a need in the group. We'll pick an issue like hiring and firing, digital footprints (branding, social media, websites), facility expansion, or multi-site strategy . . . whatever the group wants to discuss. Sometimes we keep it really simple and do on the spot coaching in each other's ministries. It is extremely effective.

The bottom line: While you may lean to one side or the other on the capital E vs. capital P question, you don't really have the luxury of staying in your *origin of leadership*. Ultimately, you have to be a little of both and be smart enough to know who you are not. So, staff to your weaknesses, cultivate relationships with other Executive Pastors and keep on learning!

Figuring Out What Kind of Executive Pastor You Are.

So how do you figure out what your *origin of leadership* is as a second-chair leader? How do you determine if you are a capital "E" **Executive** pastor or a capital "P" executive **Pastor**? My guess is that as you've read along in this chapter, you are already building a sense of where you fall. Here are some additional questions you can ask yourself to figure it out.

1. What do you love to do? It may seem like an obvious question, but how many people do what they think they *have to do*, rather than what they *love to do*? Every job will include aspects that you don't like at times, but you should never put yourself in a position where that consistently happens more than 25% of the time. I've heard pastors talk about the

things that are "life giving" vs. things that are "life draining." You want the majority of your tasks to be things that you are passionate about—things that give you life!

2. What kinds of projects do you look forward to digging into? Would you rather put time into reworking the budget spreadsheets or rethinking the way your church does pre-marital counseling? We often put off the projects we don't like. Think through the projects on your to-do list that you keep putting off. Ask yourself if those items feel more "Executive" oriented or more "Pastor" oriented. This will be very revealing.

3. Do you look forward to a day of non-stop appointments or do you simply endure it? A capital "E" guy may endure it, feeling like he's not really accomplishing anything that can be checked off a list, while a capital "P" guy may leave the office that day feeling energized and alive from all the conversations and relationship building.

4. Do you tend to hand new things off to other people fairly quickly once you are done building them or do you hold on for a long time? Capital "P" guys are tempted to hand things off too soon, which can cause problems down the road. I know that from personal experience! Capital "E" types may want to hold onto the management side of a ministry too long for fear that someone else will "screw it up." Somewhere in the middle is a better model.

5. When you think of your ideal workday or workweek, what does it look like? How much of it is spent on administration? How much of it is spent with people? How much of it is spent planning for the future of the church? How much teaching do you do? How much time is spent in general management or oversight? Just for kicks, draw out an ideal schedule. In an absolutely perfect scenario, what would your role as Executive Pastor look like on a daily basis? After you've done that, spend some time analyzing it and look for patterns that reveal your tendencies towards "E" or "P".

6. Do you find yourself saying on a regular basis, "Man, this church would run so much more smoothly if it weren't for all these people?" If so, you are probably an "E" guy—you lean on the executive side. But if you find yourself neglecting project management because you "need" to meet with people, and you enjoy those meetings, then you might lean towards the pastor side of the equation.

7. Don't assume that a guy with a primarily business background will be an E guy. Don't assume that a pastor with 20 years experience will be a P guy. I've seen it go both ways. It all comes down to strengths and weaknesses.

8. Read Tom Rath's book *Strengths Finder 2.0* and then go online and take the "Top Five" test. You will learn a great deal about yourself, and where you should be investing your personal development time. DISC, Myers-Briggs etc. are also helpful, but

Strengths Finder focuses less on personality type and more on natural talents. I found it to be more immediately helpful.

As you think through these and other questions and look hard at how God has created you, patterns should emerge that help you understand what type of Executive Pastor you are. This knowledge will allow you serve out of your strengths and appropriately augment for your weaknesses.

In the American Civil War, a guy named General Halleck functioned in a number of roles over the years, but at one point, he was essentially Abraham Lincoln's second-in-command. His title was Chief of Staff. He had some successes and some failures in that role and was not always the most personable of men. Ultimately he made the wise decision to split his job into the work of two people. Halleck became the behind the scenes guy and he let another General handle what we might call the "human side" of things. It was at that point that he found his niche and really hit his stride. He was a great systems analyst, he was great at seeing the big picture, but you really did not want him doing your yearly evaluation or managing conflict among the troops.[xx] Halleck figured out how to play to his strengths in the second-chair role and he enjoyed greater success as a result.

You know, I really believe that as pastors, we don't place enough value on the process of self-discovery and who we are in our pastoral roles. We come into ministry with pre-conceived notions of how we should spend our time based on the pastors we knew growing up, or what they told us in Bible College or seminary. I don't know how it was in your seminary, but in mine, if you were not shooting towards the lead pastor role, you were somehow *less than* others. The process of self-discovery is critical as we work through our hopes and dreams and balance them out with our gifting and skills.

Can you think of very many things that would have a bigger impact on the way you serve the church than for you to spend some significant time figuring out what kind of a pastor you are . . . what your *origin of leadership* is? If you know who are, then you know who you aren't! You may even discover that you are not an Executive Pastor! *If it really is all about the gospel, if it really is all about the mission of God, then who cares what title you have?* We need to be completely available to the mission and vision of the church so that Christ is revealed more effectively through our work *onstage as well as backstage.*

"Complementary strengths can pull in opposing and divisive directions if the relationship is not cultivated. The interaction between first and second chairs is fluid; it does not lend itself to a static job description."[xxi]

-Bonem and Patterson

CHAPTER FIVE

Towards a Job Description for the Executive Pastor

About once a month, I get an email or Facebook message with roughly the same question. It goes something like this: *"I'm new in this Executive Pastor role and no one seems to know what my job description should be, but they all know they need someone like me, what is your job description?"* Or, another version of that email comes from the Lead Pastor *"We've grown to a point where we can hire a second-in-command guy and we are trying to figure out what his job description should be, what is yours?"*

So everyone seems to know they need a guy in the #2 role, but once they get him, they don't know how he should actually spend his time. The discussion that follows inevitably falls into two categories. Either the Lead Pastor tells me that: *"A lot of stuff seems to be falling through the cracks as we get bigger. We need a detail guy."* Or the Lead Pastor says: *"I have this vision for the church that I feel like God has laid on my heart, but I have a hard time figuring out how to get there. I need someone who can figure out the steps."* The other concern I hear a lot is related to trust: *"I need another pastor that I can trust with anything in the church. I need to know that if I give this guy the* membership class, he can lead it well, and I won't have to do damage control later on," or, "I want to know that when I go away on vacation, everything will be taken care of and that if an emergency comes up, there is someone else who can handle it, and maybe even preach for me." It all boils down to this pain point on the part of the Lead Pastor: "**I need a trusted right-hand man. I need a true partner in ministry.**"

So how do you come up with a job description for a guy whose stated purpose in your church is to fill in the cracks of leadership and take partially formed ideas and bring them into reality? Well . . . you don't! Unlike almost any other job in the church, *the definition of an Executive Pastor inherently lacks definition.* It is perennially undefined. While my basic job has not changed the entire time I've been an Executive Pastor, the outworking of that job is a moving target and always has been.

Bennett and Miles, in speaking of the corporate world say it this way: *"There is no agreed-on description of what the job contains, what it entails, or what it is called. As one executive shared with us, "You can define the job any way you feel like, depending upon the individuals and what you are trying to accomplish." Robert Herbold, who served as COO at Microsoft, told us he doesn't "think there is a single thing as a role called 'chief operating officer.'"* Instead, he commented that "there is a constellation of responsibilities that can be put together to create a job that easily carries that title."[xxii] That said, even though explaining the daily out-workings of the Executive Pastor role is a moving target, it *is* possible to speak intelligently about the big picture in a way that remains somewhat constant.

VERY BROADLY STATED . . .

In my first role as an Executive Pastor at Terra Nova Church in NY, my Lead Pastor, Ed Marcelle said this during a coaching session with another LP/XP team: "XP's are the men who take the raw material of a visionary's hazy dreams and form it into a movement".[xxiii] With that in mind, if you boil my job down to it's most basic component it would read something like this:

Phil Taylor's job is to "intre"preneurally oversee the effective implementation of his church's vision, which is largely the vision of his Lead Pastor.

Now, I'll take some time to break this down part by part.

WHAT DO I MEAN BY "INTRE"PENEUR?[xxiv]

We all know that an entrepreneur is someone who loves to start new things and can't help but come up with ideas that seemingly no one has ever thought of. In a Lead Pastor, this entrepreneurial spirit pairs well with the need to create and cast a clear vision for where the church is headed. What is frequently missed is the idea that a great vision often has a hard time getting off the ground because the visionary may not be sure how to make it happen. He came up with the idea, he knows what the finished product should look like, but the in-between is foggy at best. Bringing vision into reality requires an intre-preneur, someone who can take a basic idea or visionary concept and bring it to life. This act, in and of itself, requires a certain *type* of visioneering and entrepreneurial skill. It requires a self-starter, not a workhorse who just follows the path laid out for him. It requires a chameleon pastor who can move back and forth from vision to implementation, from dreaming to doing, back and forth, back and forth, all day long.

I love how this struggle is worded in *Leading From the Second Chair*: *"The unique tensions for a second chair arise because the expectations he encounters appear to be incompatible, or even contradictory. He is expected to be a bold initiator and faithful follower, a creative thinker and detailed implementer."*[xxv] One of my absolute favorite books on the second-chair role comes from the secular business world. You've probably never heard of it, but you should go read it (at least read the first half). It's called *Riding Shotgun: The Role of the COO*. The authors nail this issue so well that even though the book is written for the business world, its insights on the second-chair role apply easily to the church. Listen to authors Bennett & Miles:

"Many people view the CEO role as being more about strategy and the future and the COO role as being more about today's operations. However, a COO who is not capable of strategic thinking is a disaster. You have to be able to think strategically in order to implement."[xxvi]

I am convinced that there are a lot of great XPs hiding out in LP jobs because they think that if they leave the LP role, they won't get to be creative anymore, dreaming up new ideas and plans. Just the opposite is true! I have worked with two great visionary entrepreneurial Lead Pastors who have given me the freedom and energy to dream up wonderfully creative solutions to needs in the church and strategies to implement new ideas. In this type of trusting environment, the interaction between LP and XP will feed that discovery process back and forth. Having the starting point somewhat defined in advance by the LP will give the XP the freedom to soar and create something special without the need for a ton of oversight from the LP. I'm not the guy who gives birth to the original vision. I'm the guy who takes a great idea and makes it even better by wrapping it up all snug and warm with systems, structures, and strategies to ensure that the great idea makes it into the real world, which benefits real people throughout the church and beyond.

Let me give you an example. When I arrived at Mosaic Church in Orlando, FL, I asked our Lead Pastor, Renaut VanDerRiet, what the biggest need in the church was. He said "If we don't get Leadership Development right really soon, we'll never move on to the next chapter of our life as a church." That's pretty much all he said on that subject. Out of that conversation, I dedicated a significant amount of time in my first year to developing an in-depth leadership development strategy that fit with the existing DNA and rhythms of the church. At key points in the development process, I showed Renaut what I was working on to make sure he was comfortable with the direction I was headed, but for the most part I had freedom to lead steps 2 through 99. You see, the core vision provided by Renaut was that "we need more and better leaders" if we are really going to change the world, but after that, I had great freedom to creatively develop things as I saw fit. I'm not a visionary entrepreneur, but I still need to have some "visionary" in me to do my job well. I have to be an *"intre"preneur*.

WHAT DO I MEAN BY "OVERSEE"?

What did I say my job description is again? *Phil Taylor's job is to "intre"preneurally oversee the effective implementation of his church's vision, which is largely the vision of his Lead Pastor.*

So, what do I mean by "oversee"? Simply put, I mean that I don't really "do" much, I just make sure that a lot gets done. I spend a lot of time connecting with the people who are further out on the front lines than I am. There are times at the end of a busy day where I ask myself, "What did I even do today?" I look back at the staff meeting with 50 people, the one on one meeting with the campus pastor, the catalyst meeting with the team in charge of some project and the 15 little unplanned, unscheduled meetings that happen when I am just *physically present* in the building, a day where I barely had time to check email and definitely did not check a single thing off a list and I ask myself "what did I actually do today"? Well, what I did was *oversee* a crap-load of stuff!

It would be so nice at times to narrowly define what I do into a predictable pattern of repeatable tasks, but that is not a luxury that a Second-Chair Pastor has. If an XP is living like that, he is not an XP. He might be an OP (Operations Pastor), or an EA (Executive Assistant to the LP). Both are incredibly important jobs in churches that are large enough to have them. But Executive Pastors need to have a high tolerance for both complexity and ambiguity. If you need everything written down and locked down in order to be comfortable with the job, you probably should not be an XP.

Here's the thing: all those meetings I referred to in a typical day actually lead to exponential impact that ripples out for weeks on end, maybe even months or years! A one-hour meeting with one of our campus pastors may result in 20 hours of work on his end to move his ministry forward. A two-hour meeting casting vision and direction with a team that has been assembled for a particular project may result in 200 hours of work on the part of that team. Bonem and Patterson say it this way: *"A person who is able to succeed by influencing others is a more effective leader than one who issues edicts to be obeyed."xxvii* It's true— Executive Pastors don't do much, but we have the incredible privilege and responsibility to ensure that much gets done.

And yet, there are typically 2-3 projects at a time that I do have my sleeves rolled up for. Bonem and Patterson's comment on this reality is so helpful: *"Being in the second chair is the ultimate leadership paradox. It is the paradox of . . . having a deep role and a wide one, and being content with the present while continuing to dream about the future."xxviii* There is a period of time at the beginning of a new project where I am very hands-on in the creation and structure-building process. It then becomes my primary task to train up a replacement in that area (volunteer or staff) and clear that project from my plate to make room for the next piece of vision that needs to be implemented. This has continued to shift as I've traveled through different church sizes and seasons. In my early days of church planting, I spent a lot of time directly leading the "doers." Today I spend most of my time leading the "leaders," who in turn, lead the "doers." In some cases, I'm leading the leaders who lead the leaders who lead the doers. (Yes, it can be that complicated.) In the midst of those shifts, it's critical that I keep my ear to the ground by intentionally connecting with all levels of leadership, paid and unpaid, on a regular basis. Keeping this kind of pulse on the church allows me to lead effectively.

I had the privilege of attending a business conference put on by the Walt Disney Company through their *Disney Institute*. It was called *"Disney's Approach To Creativity and Innovation."* One maxim that Disney management lives by is to *"Over-manage the details that everyone else under-manages".* [xxix] Disney World does this by caring about trash can design and landscaping and the way a ride smells on a hot summer afternoon in Florida. Executive Pastors can do this by seeing how the various parts of the church inter-relate and by being ready to step in anywhere and everywhere as needed just to cause little course corrections as we bring vision into reality. This is what it means to *oversee* as a second-chair leader. You *see over* everything all at once. Note that over-managing is very different than micro-managing. You don't have time to micro-manage, and if you do, the church will probably outgrow you at some point soon. As Executive Pastors, we have to be aware of the weeds, but not get caught up in them. Lean on your trusted direct reports and then get the heck out of their way!

WHAT DO I MEAN BY "EFFECTIVE IMPLEMENTATION"?

Once again, *Phil Taylor's job is to "intre"preneurally oversee the effective implementation of his church's vision, which is largely the vision of his Lead Pastor.*

So what does it mean to "effectively implement"? It means getting the job done, and getting it done well so that your LP is not worrying about the details on Sunday morning or any other day of the week for that matter. The LP should not need to constantly step in on issues well removed from those who directly report to him, and if you are training up and equipping the right team, neither should you. Your LP did his job in carefully selecting a good XP to oversee the effective implementation of the vision. Now it's your job to take his ideas in their most basic, unrefined and undefined form and reverse-engineer them to figure out how to bring that vision into reality for the church or the community. Every good idea is execution dependent. The business world knows this, and the church needs to learn it as well. As Eric Geiger said on his blog, *"An executive pastor who cannot execute is a painfully ironic oxymoron."*xxx

Effectively implementing a vision potentially involves a million details and a ton of people. Depending on the size and scope of each piece of the vision, you may need timelines, budgets and capital campaigns, a team of volunteers or staff, graphic and promotional support, a communication plan, multiple catalyst meetings, facility reservations or even renovations, hospitality, security, tech support, and on and on it goes. Along the way, you will continually be called in for clarification. Implementation *is* clarification! Implementation inherently involves continual clarification.

Strategically Deploying Your Lead Pastor in Vision Implementation

When you are implementing vision, it's important to ask where you can deploy your Lead Pastor strategically. Even though he is your boss, he is also a resource to be spent for the cause of Christ. Your Lead Pastor may function like a consultant on a particular project, checking back in here and there to make sure you and the team are on the right track, or he may have a piece of the job assigned back to him. You may call on him to communicate key points of the vision along the journey of implementation because he is likely your best communicator. If your Lead Pastor understands the concept of mutual submission, he will trust and respect your wisdom on when and where to best utilize his skill set and voice.

There is a great story about Walt Disney as he was beginning work on California's Disneyland in the post-war era. While various artists were taking his ideas and turning them into concept drawings, Walt engaged the famed architect Welton Becket with the intention of handing off the vast majority of the early design of Disneyland to outside architecture firms. Becket, who was a friend of Walt's, refused, telling Walt that only Walt Disney could design Disneyland, meaning that no one else could see it like he saw it. It needed his fingerprints stamped all over it if it was going to capture his heart and spirit.[xxxi]

Executive Pastors will do well to strategically ask for their Lead Pastor's engagement early on for certain types of projects. Your LP may have great trust in your ability to execute the development of a new ministry or project and will be inclined to step away early on and say "You've got this," and you may feel like you are helping him by taking something off of his shoulders. But there are times when the wisest move for the church is to keep your LP engaged for a little while longer during the early design phase to make sure things are really moving in the right direction. Then, when you are confident that you understand his vision, free him up to move onto other needs.

Deploying your Lead Pastor strategically gets easier as you develop mutual trust. As I gained a greater understanding of Renaut's vision for Mosaic Church and the gap between where we were and where we wanted to be, I spoke into the teaching calendar (which is actually overseen by a different pastor on our teaching team), and I suggested that we needed to do a month-long series about what it means to be Mosaic Church to help define and clarify where we were headed as a community.[xxxii] I knew that no matter how well written a document or blog post was, it ultimately needed to come out of our Lead Pastor's mouth for the people to really get behind it.

The nature of this sermon series required input from a dozen key players on our team and because it involved the communication of more details than is typical for Renaut, it also meant creating talking points on key issues for him to hit in each sermon. On one week of the series, we were articulating our hopes for Missional Communities more clearly than ever before, so we asked our Discipleship Pastor to gather talking points, key phrases and important data for that weekends teaching and coach the Lead Pastor. On another week, we were launching our new Eldership Development program and introducing our existing Elders to the church in a more formal manner. Because we have seven services a weekend, it seemed easier to make a video that could then have a long shelf life on our website's leadership page after being used in the sermon itself. I literally wrote the script for Renaut and everyone else who spoke on camera. You cannot put words in a person's mouth if they don't trust you! On our final week, we were rolling out Covenant Partnership in a church where membership had previously consisted of slapping a bumper sticker of our logo on your car and saying "I'm in!" Therefore, this final sermon involved multiple meetings with the Elders and key staff to make sure that the language we chose struck just the right tone and didn't freak people out. Do you see all the steps and details needed for a project like this one month sermon series?

Let me quickly re-cap the flowchart of this particular project for you.

1. The Lead Pastor dreams up a vision.

2. The Executive Pastor sketches out the components needed to bring said vision into reality.

3. Lots more people get involved in the details related to each portion of each component of the vision.

4. The Executive Pastor and others on the team go back to the Lead Pastor and bring him up to speed on the details of this particular vision implementation.

5. The Lead Pastor uses his primary gifting as a communicator to tell the congregation not only what the vision is, but how we are going to bring it into reality.

6. The congregation is excited and energized and has a clear sense of what they should do next.

In order to effectively implement one unified vision, lots of people needed to be involved in refining and contextualizing that vision throughout the church. When our leadership teams are willing to submit to one other, we not only make Jesus happy with our unity, we get the job done better and faster. Just like any good marriage, mutual submission is key to successfully bringing vision into reality. Effective implementation is the biggest understatement in my self-made job description, and it's where I spend most of my time.

Side Note About Protecting the Vision . . .

Implementing a vision is not a "one and done" kind of thing like building an addition onto your house or playing a game with your kids. It's more like planting a tree that will require continual care and nurturing over the years. When you bring a vision into reality, it becomes a living thing in the hearts and minds of your staff and your congregation. As such, the purity and clarity of the vision needs to be protected. When it existed in the mind of your Lead Pastor, it was pure, even if it was unformed. When you, and others tasked with bringing that vision into reality, actually succeeded in *bringing it into reality*, it suddenly had dozens, perhaps hundreds of people looking at it, questioning it, tweaking it, improving it, and morphing it! A certain amount of adjustment is helpful and appropriate, but too much can take the vision off course.

The XP is in a unique position to protect the vision. In many churches with XPs, there are only really two people who have the *positional authority* to speak into literally anything and everything and say "No, we are not doing that, because it does not fit with our core vision." Speaking to the corporate world, Bennet and Miles say it this way: "COO's occupy a position that is unique structurally, strategically, socially, and politically."[xxxiii]

The simple reality of human nature is that you may have people on your staff or in high level's of leadership who will have their own mission/vision (read: agenda). Some may be acting in the flesh. Others may be innocently mistaking their own passions for the churches vision and projecting that into their spheres of influence. Whatever the motivation, before you know it, you'll have one department charging forward in one direction and another department charging forward in another direction. Suddenly you are square in the middle of mission creep and vision drift. It is the job of the XP to step in and say, "Listen, what you are desiring is not wrong, it's just not the mission of this church, so we simply cannot resource it with the church's money or your time." This happens in casual conversations and official review meetings. It happens when budget requests are made, and it happens after the fact when someone has run ahead of themselves and built something that now has to be disassembled so as not to distract from the true vision. Saying "no" is usually harder than saying "yes," but it often has a far greater impact on the success of the church.

Perhaps the most difficult place to protect the vision is with your visionary Lead Pastor! I love this quote from Eisner's book "Working Together": *"My life is entrepreneurial. But the entrepreneur has a weakness, and the entrepreneur's weakness is that they know no boundaries, they don't know any restraints. And so I always say, if you're an entrepreneur, you've got to find yourself somebody who is financially oriented, and whose judgement you can trust. You don't let them stop you—you only let them slow you down. That is really what you need."* [xxxiv]

I have had the privilege of working with two great, entrepreneurial, big-vision types of Lead Pastors. They are a unique breed of humans. The stream of new ideas is never ending! Sometimes those new ideas augment and expand the core vision, but other times, those new ideas are just shiny little distractions along the road. If you have the trust and respect of your Lead Pastor, you'll be able to speak into these ideas with a great set of questions to figure out which type of idea you are dealing with. Done correctly, you'll be able to help your LP stay focused on *his own* big vision. I'll expand much more on the relationship between the LP and the XP in the next book in this series. [xxxv]

What do I mean by "his churches vision—which is largely the vision of his lead pastor?"

Remember the job description? *Phil Taylor's job is to "intre"preneurally oversee the effective implementation of his church's vision, which is largely the vision of his Lead Pastor.*

The Lead Pastor *has to* chart the overall vision for the church. This happens in a million different ways, but the vision must begin with him. The only way that I as XP can make sure that the vision is being implemented well is to know that vision and internalize it as well as my LP has. This requires hours upon hours of time with the LP gaining a clear sense of his vision for the church, both the initial driving vision for the church, as well as the newly cast vision that continues to roll out each year. It requires asking a million follow-up questions and poking holes in the vision in an effort to sharpen your understanding of it.

The reason why Titus made such a good partner for Paul is because he was eager to see the mission of God develop. He believed in it just as much as Paul did. If you are not all-out ready to implement the vision of the Lead Pastor, you will not be a good partner for him. You have to want it just as bad as he does.

Some people are called to be a voice, and some people are called to be an echo, and that's ok.[xxxvi] Unlike a worship pastor or youth pastor, who could potentially have the exact same job description while working for two *very* different Lead Pastors, the XP necessarily takes his cues from his LP for what projects take center stage, what gifts and abilities of his move into the spotlight, and therefore, it is impossible to craft the Second Chair Pastor's job description without first defining the LP's Job Description. The more that the XP's gifts, abilities, personality type and temperament are *unlike* the LP's, the better, as this allows for balancing one another out. Finding the right fit for both is critical.

Special Note for Lead Pastors:

Lead Pastors, I would encourage you to spend some time writing out what your **real** job is right now. In other words, how do you **actually** spend your time? Then, write out where you want that to be in a couple of years. In other words, how do you **want** to spend your time in the future? Call out the items that are sucking you dry that you **have to** get off of your plate (be very specific). Look for the patterns in those items (people?, details?, management?, research?) and look for an XP who can adequately alleviate you of at least some of those items now, while working towards the rest over time. Your future XP does not have to be an expert at those things, but he does have to be an expert at finding and resourcing and managing people (both leaders & doers) who are experts at those things. Once you have a clear sense of where you want your LP job description to go in the coming years, you will be able to figure out how to define or refine your XP's job description more effectively.

"The reason I left you in Crete was that you might straighten out what was left unfinished and appoint elders in every town, as I directed you."

1 Timothy 1:5

Conclusion

Did you ever actually define the Executive Pastor Role?

Now that you're at the conclusion of the book, you might ask, "Wait, did he ever actually define Executive Pastor role?" The truth is... no, not really. Sorry about that. Maybe you can ask Amazon for your money back. Don't email me though. I've already spent your money on half of a latte at Starbucks.

Here's the deal—you can't really define the XP role. You can't really write a proper and simple job description for the second-chair role unless it's really vague like mine. All you can really do is speak about the "shifting sands" nature of the role and say "good luck, bro!" Thankfully, a good XP can do almost any job in the church moderately well in a pinch, because good XPs are the kinds of people who, when they see a need, or a leadership vacuum, roll up their sleeves and get to work. They can't even help it really!

Warren Buffet, the famous and incredibly rich investor said this about Charlie Munger, his second-in-command, *"Charlie can't encounter a problem without thinking of an answer. He has the best thirty-second mind I've ever seen. I'll call him up, and within thirty seconds, he'll grasp it. He just sees things immediately.* "xxxvii Bringing it back to the church, a good XP doesn't worry about his past experience in the particular area of the church with a current need. For example, you may find yourself launching a small groups ministry even though you've never really done that before. Suddenly UPS is at your doorstep with boxes of books you've ordered from Amazon and you are reading everything you can find on models of small group ministry. You are calling up friends at other churches and picking their brains; you are reaching out to pastors who are known experts in small groups, missional communities, etc. and setting up Facetime/Skype calls or even getting on a plane to go to a conference or training. You are taking notes, forming ideas, bringing together teams of people and interfacing with key staff and lay leaders. It doesn't matter that you have never launched or re-launched a small groups ministry at a church before. You went "back to school" so to speak, and you became an expert.

I've seen XPs filling in as Worship Pastors, Lead Pastors, Children's Ministry Pastors, you name it! My good friend and fellow XP Scott Fischer said it this way in a conversation one day at an XP Roundtable I was hosting: *"I didn't necessarily set out to be an XP, I just started filling in the gaps."* xxxviii

This is the hallmark of a good XP: the ability to jump into just about any role and do it moderately well. Is there someone better for the job? Probably, and that's why you will ultimately hand it off to someone else. But sometimes the best person for the job is the person who has both the time and the drive to call something new into existence coupled with a deep understanding and commitment to the Lead Pastor's vision. You may be the only person in your church that fits that definition. Executive Pastors are like utility players. *The best right hand men are actually ambidextrous.*

So you see, there is no real definition of an Executive Pastor except those written in chalk that can be easily wiped clean and re-written as needed. If you have the intangible qualities that make a great XP, you'll find that truth to be an exciting challenge that will keep you busy for years to come.

Bibliography

Ambrose, Stephen E. *Halleck: Lincoln's Chief of Staff*. Louisiana: Louisiana State University Press, 1996.

Bennett, Nathan and Stephen A. Miles. *Riding Shotgun: The Role of the COO*. Stanford, CA: Stanford University Press, 2006.

Bonem, Mike and Roger Patterson. *Leading From the Second Chair: Serving Your Church, Fulfilling Your Role and Realizing Your Dreams*. San Francisco, CA: Jossey-Bass Publishers, 2005.

Eisner, Michael D. and Aaron R. Cohen. *Working Together: Why Great Partnerships Succeed*. HarperBusiness, New York, 2012.

Geiger, Eric. "XP1: Executive Pastor Tension," ericgeiger.com, accessed October 5, 2012, http://ericgeiger.com/2011/11/xp-1-executive-pastor-tension.php.

"XP5: Leading Up (Deliver Results)," ericgeiger.com, accessed October 5, 2012, http://ericgeiger.com/2011/12/xp-5-leading-up-deliver-results.php.

Hornsby, Billy. *Success for the Second in Command: Leading from the Second   Chariot*. Lake Mary, FL: Creation House, 2005.

Patterson, Roger. *Theology of the Second Chair*. Lulu.com, 2011.

Rath, Tom. *Strengths Finder 2.0* Gallup Press, New York, 2007.

Strauch, Alexander. *Biblical Eldership: An Urgent Call to Restore Biblical   Church Leadership*. Colorado Springs, CO: Lewis and Roth Publishers,   1995.

Thomas, Bob. *Building a Company: Roy O. Disney and the Creation of an   Entertainment Empire*. New York: Disney Editions, 1998.

About the Author

Phil is a graduate of Cairn University and Dallas Theological Seminary and has served the church for over twenty years. He is passionate about bringing vision into reality and has spent the last ten years serving alongside of gifted communicator-visionary *Lead Pastors* of Acts 29 Network churches in New York and, more recently in Florida where he now serves as the Executive Pastor of Leadership and Development at Mosaic, a multi-site church in West Orlando and at Walt Disney World. (www.thisismosaic.org) Phil loves reading, researching, writing, running and kayaking. He has been married to Aimee since 2002. They live west of Orlando, Florida with their three children and one cat.

Contacting the Author

For speaking, consulting or coaching requests, please email: backstagepastors@gmail.com .

Social Media

Twitter: @philtaylorxp

Instagram: @philtaylorxp

Facebook: facebook.com/philtaylorxp

For articles and additional information from the author, such as upcoming speaking engagements or new books, visit www.backstagepastors.com .

Acknowledgements

I feel like acknowledgements belong at the end of a book, not the beginning. More like the credits at the end of a movie. That's why you find them here. To start, I need to thank the people that helped make this book legible and coherent. Sean Nolan helped with some of my research while interning with me. Lisa Gilbert edited an earlier version of *Backstage Pastors* when it was going to be one long-form book instead of several smaller books. Leon Hayduchok edited the book for content and Jimmy Hoang gave it the final grammar, spelling and punctuation edit. Keith Winter did the cover art and Jeff Amato consulted on the creation of the associated website, backstagepastors.org. John Stange helped me navigate the world of Kindle Publishing. And of course, Mike Bonem so graciously wrote my forward. Truthfully, this book stands on the shoulders of Mike's book *Leading from the Second Chair*.

In addition to these obvious players, there are countless other pastors, mentors, friends and family that have contributed to my development and made me who I am. I'll call attention to just a few. My parents and my brothers created an environment that allowed me to explore ministry options in the churches where my dad pastored. During my years at Cairn University (formerly known as Philadelphia Biblical University), Todd Williams and Cam Garven were my biggest influences. My years at Dallas Seminary were given definition through my church involvement under George Hillman's direction as my ministry mentor. Ed Marcelle has been a part of my life as a pastor since the early 2000's. I had the privilege of taking over his first church plant (King's Chapel) as Lead Pastor, and later planting Terra Nova Church alongside of him in NY. His early trust in my untested ability created the petri dish that I needed to grow into the Executive Pastor that I am. Renaut Van der Riet took a chance on me, believing that I had the ability to lead a much larger church than the one I was in when I became the Executive Pastor at Mosaic Church in Orlando. David Fletcher, Mike Bonem and Bill Minchin were three XP's that invested in me early on. As always, there are countless others that I could mention.

The staff at both Terra Nova Church and Mosaic Church have been incredibly supportive of my desire to write and create resources that are laser-focused on Second Chair Leaders. The XP roundtables that I have been a part of and the many conferences that I've spoken at have created an environment to field-test material before putting it to print.

More than anyone else, I have to thank my wife Aimee and my three kids for freeing me up to write and seeing it as an important part of my calling to give God the greatest return on the investments He has made in my life. They made sacrifices so that you could have this book in your possession. Ultimately, all glory and honor go to God.

ENDNOTES

[i] Hornsby, Billy. *Success for the Second in Command : Leading from the Second Chariot.* Lake Mary, FL: Creation House, 2005. P. vii

[ii] Patterson, Roger, *Theology of the Second Chair.* P.29-31

[iii] The two very clear exceptions to this lack of resources must be acknowledged up front both for their quality of content and impact on my own thinking. Mike Bonem and Roger Patterson wrote the seminal book on the XP role entitled *"Leading from the Second Chair".* Seriously, you need to read it. Additionally, David Fletcher has hosted a yearly gathering for executive pastors in Dallas for nearly a decade and has made himself incredibly available to pastors all around the world. Find his website and annual conference at xpastor.org.

[iv] Kyle Nabors from Kensington Church in Detroit, Michigan.

[v] The Acts 29 Church Planting Network, based in Dallas, TX at The Village Church. www.acts29network.org

[vi] Ambrose, Stephen E. *Halleck: Lincoln's Chief of Staff.* p.11

[vii] Thank you to my former Lead Pastor Ed Marcelle for saying this about yourself countless times. www.terranovachurch.org

[viii] Stated by Bryce Butler in the XP track at the 2009 Acts29 boot camp at Sojourn on a panel led by Bryce Butler (former XP of Sojourn Louisville), Jamie Munson (formerly of the late Mars Hill Church, Seattle), Kevin Peck (Second Chair leader at Austin Stone Church) and myself.

[ix] Bonem, Mike and Roger Patterson, *Leading From The Second Chair: Serving Your Church, Fulfilling Your Role and Realizing Your Dreams.* P.2

[x] Geiger, Eric, "XP1: Executive Pastor Tension." Blog, accessed on Oct. 5th, 2012 http://ericgeiger.com/2011/11/xp-1-executive-pastor-tension.php

[xi] Alexander Strauch's book *Biblical Eldership: An Urgent Call To Restore Biblical Church Leadership* is the most comprehensive look at this topic. I cannot recommend it highly enough.

[xii] Rath, Tom. *Strengths Finder 2.0 p. 18*

[xiii] Interestingly, there was a survey done a couple of years ago on XPs by the Leadership Network. The asked nearly 600 Executive Pastors a number of questions including questions of previous work experience. They found that 70% had five years of full time experience outside the church. Of that 70%, 55% came from the business world, 9% came from a job in education, and 5% from the military.

[xiv] True story. Thankfully not about me.

[xv] Ed Marcelle at Terra Nova Church, Troy, NY. But honestly, Ed is much better with people than he gives himself credit for!

[xvi] Book Two of the Backstage Pastors series deals with the Relationship between the Lead Pastor and the Executive Pastor in much more depth.

[xvii] This is from a conversation with Kyle Nabors from Kensington Church in Detroit, Michigan.

[xviii] Many thanks to Bill Minchin at Grace Fellowship Church of Watervliet, NY who poured hours into me as I poured cups of coffee into him at the Daily Grind in Troy, NY. www.gracefellowship.com

[xix] *The Lego Movie*. Thanks to my six year old boy Simon for drilling that song deep, deep into my brain.

[xx] Ambrose, Stephen E. *Halleck: Lincoln's Chief of Staff.*—p.47

[xxi] Bonem, Mike and Roger Patterson, *Leading From The Second*

Chair: Serving Your Church, Fulfilling Your Role and Realizing Your Dreams. (Kindle Locations 487-488). Kindle Edition.

xxii Bennett, Nathan and Stephen A. Miles. *Riding Shotgun: The Role of the COO*. P. 63

xxiii Ed Marcelle in a conversation with another Lead Pastor who was seeking our advice.

xxiv I was pretty sure that I coined this phrase "intre-preneur" until I did a google search and found that half a dozen others were using it as well. That said, I have yet to find someone using it in the way that I use it here. So there, let the lawsuits commence.

xxv Bonem, Mike and Roger Patterson. *Leading From The Second Chair: Serving Your Church, Fulfilling Your Role and Realizing Your Dreams*. (Kindle Locations 167-168). Kindle Edition.

xxvi Bennett, Nathan and Stephen A. Miles. *Riding Shotgun: The Role of the COO*. P.99

xxvii Bonem, Mike and Roger Patterson. *Leading From The Second Chair: Serving Your Church, Fulfilling Your Role and Realizing Your Dreams*. (Kindle Locations 149-151). Kindle Edition.

xxviii Bonem, Mike and Roger Patterson. *Leading From The Second Chair: Serving Your Church, Fulfilling Your Role and Realizing Your Dreams*. (Kindle Locations 110-111). Kindle Edition.

xxix Disney Institute. *Disney's Approach To Creativity and Innovation*. May, 2014

xxx Geiger, Eric, "XP5: Leading Up (Deliver Results)." Blog, accessed on Oct. 5th, 2012, http://ericgeiger.com/2011/12/xp-5-leading-up-deliver-results.php

xxxi Thomas, Bob. *Building a Company: Roy O. Disney and the Creation of an Entertainment Empire*. P.182

xxxii If you are curious, you can find this series called "This Is The Church" on Mosaic Church's website http://thisismosaic.org/media/messages/series/this-is-the-church/

xxxiii Bennett, Nathan and Stephen A. Miles. *Riding Shotgun: The Role of the COO.* P.1

xxxiv Bernie Marcus in *Working Together: Why Great Partnerships Succeed.* P.176

xxxv Look for the next book in late 2015ish or early 2016.

xxxvi I heard my friend and fellow author/pastor, JR Vassar say something like this in a conversation. Exact quote and context is too far in the past to remember.

xxxvii Eisner, Michael D. and Aaron R. Cohen. *Working Together: Why Great Partnerships Succeed.* P.39

xxxviii Scott Fischer is the Executive Pastor at Temple Baptist Church in Halfmoon, NY and an author with eciple.com.

Made in the USA
Lexington, KY
14 September 2018